over the roofs of the world

Also by the author:

poetry
Talking of Trees
Gardening in the Tropics

short fiction
Summer Lightning
Arrival of the Snake-Woman
Discerner of Hearts

non-fiction
A-Z of Jamaican Heritage
Working Miracles: Women's Lives in the English-Speaking Caribbean
Encyclopedia of Jamaican Heritage

over the roofs of the world

Olive Senior

A 4 A.M. BOOK

INSOMNIAC PRESS

Library and Archives Canada Cataloguing in Publication

Senior, Olive
 Over the roofs of the world / Olive Senior.

Poems.
ISBN 1-894663-82-9

 I. Title.

PS8587.E552O94 2005   C811'.54   C2005-900249-2

The publisher gratefully acknowledges the support of the Canada Council, the Ontario Arts Council and the Department of Canadian Heritage through the Book Publishing Industry Development Program.

Printed and bound in Canada

Insomniac Press
192 Spadina Avenue, Suite 403
Toronto, Ontario, Canada, M5T 2C2
www.insomniacpress.com

THE CANADA COUNCIL | LE CONSEIL DES ARTS
FOR THE ARTS | DU CANADA
SINCE 1957 | DEPUIS 1957

ONTARIO ARTS COUNCIL
CONSEIL DES ARTS DE L'ONTARIO

For those who've travelled . . .
John, Elsa, Gloria and Herman

TABLE OF CONTENTS

THE PULL OF BIRDS

Colón, son and grand-son of weavers
        rejected that calling but did not
                neglect craft (keeping two sets of books).
        On his first voyage, landfall receding
        (where was Japan?) he sailed on

praying for a miracle to centre him
        in that unmarked immensity, as warp to woof.
        And suddenly from the north a density
                of birds flying south, their autumn migration
                intersecting his westward passage.

At such an auspicious conjunction, his charts
        he threw out, the flocks drew him south
        across the blue fabric of the Atlantic.
                Weary mariners buoyed by the miracle
                        of land soon, of birds flying across the moon.

Birds seeking to outdistance three raptors skimming
                        the surface of the sea and sending skyward
                        their doomsday utterance of hawks' bells
                                tinkling endlessly. Birds speeding
                                        to make landfall at Guanahaní.

1: A LITTLE BIRD TOLD ME . . .

The Secret of Capturing Parrot

Up in the tree, wild Parrot sinks into the green canopy
and mimics silence. Speech comes only when spoken to.
His captors use smoke to draw him in: pimento wood and
resin on a fire built under the tree Parrot is perched in.
They'll sit and wait till Parrot is stunned enough to drop.

 How will they know where Parrot is hiding?

The wind shifts.
      Parrot's captors break out in a fit of coughing.

          Coughing
                unleashes
                      Parrot's tongue.

THE SECRET OF TAMING PARROT

Wild Parrot can be tamed
    By gently blowing
        Tobacco smoke
            Over its beak
                And laughing.

THE SECRET OF TURNING GREEN PARROT YELLOW

The secret of that outward transformation
      comes
            from within.

Defeathered and rubbed with Toad's blood,
      Green Parrot
            grows new feathers

of a red or yellow hue.
      (Others claim that making Parrot eat the fat
            of certain fish will do.)

Humans use Parrot feathers
      to transform themselves
            from the outside in.

But what does Toad have to say? Was it millennia of hope
that evolved its blood as the perfect medium for heightening
Parrot's display? Or were the blood ties always there? Have
amphibia been harbouring a secret desire for uplift ever since
they watched their bird cousins soar away? Does Toad hope
Parrot will one day leak the secret of flight, of speech,
of colour, to its blood?

THE SECRET OF FLYING CLOSE TO THE SUN WITHOUT MELTING WINGS

Discard the illusion of bearing yourself up. Only Bird,
     Sun's messenger, can transport you. This is not
        about wings of power

(that will burn, melt) but the power of wings lent to you
     by Grandfather Macaw. *If* he chooses
        to hear you.

Know that you come into the world featherless
     and naked. Like an egg. A cypher.
        Grandfather might permit you to pluck

one set of feathers to dress yourself in. Lend you hollow
     bones (to be returned after flight); breathe you into
        the lightness of air. (The feathers you might

be allowed to keep for many lifetimes). To prepare, know
     it is not a question of artifice but of becoming.
        Not build up but strip down. To dress up

you need the feathers, the paint, the beads, the flowers.
     The hallucinogenic rhythm of the rattles, the
        drums, your steed.

Power will come not swiftly on the wing but feather out of
     the homage.The humility. The loving
        preparation.The desire

to transform into Other. Leading to that auspicious moment:
     the whirr of wings speak plain. You have entered
        that place where flight is a given.

For you, flight is given as gift of bird messenger sustained
by rattle, by drum, by song. You soar, sail, glide.
For a brief moment you gain Sun's nod.

You are Bird itself. But know: such ecstasy is not forever.
You will re-enter your world, but let down lightly
cradled as gently as egg.

THE SECRET OF CRUSOE'S PARROT

Parrot through heavily-lidded eyes, watches as the new
   invader arrives. Friend or foe? Parrot doesn't know,
     doesn't care. Parrot is ruler of air.

This island kingdom was Parrot's from time immemorial,
   before arrivals, departures, of many such as he.
     Their claims of overlordship

as predictable as the tide. Parrot's weakness is that he
   loves company; even a human will do.
     Parrot is all pretence, mimicry,

playing fool to catch wise. Yet if Crusoe had asked, Parrot
   would have told no lies; he'd seen it all before.
     Could have told where the fresh springs were;

how to bake bread, set traps, fire pottery. Where best
   to build the boat. But (Parrot thinks) I mustn't gloat
     for then I would have deprived

the poor creature of his illusion of mastery, and myself
   of some good jokes. Such as his thinking
     I'm alone and celibate. *Poor Poll*

says he. *You are just like me.* Not knowing what lurks
   disguised as sweet juicy fruit in yonder tree –
     My mate. My progeny.

I let him teach me speech for much I forget between visitors.
   And granted that such speech as I usually
     imbibe – from cannibals, pirates

buccaneers, delirious castaways, is not appropriate
for his Christian ears. Though sometimes
when I'm angry or for mischief

I let fly a few. He usually attributes these to his loneliness
and delirium; or to his mishearing. He prays
extra hard those nights.

"Poor Robin Crusoe," I mock him. "Where have you been?
How come you here?" *Poll*, he claims loftily, *the
only person permitted to talk to me.*

His servant, indeed. When that other creature came, the
one called Friday, I almost left him (that one was
a quick study. Knew exactly how

to please). I stayed because being 'Crusoe's parrot' does
give me status among the poor dumb creatures
in the trees. Now their teacher is me.

I had thought of peopling the island with educated parrots
and sweet airs. But I laid off the teaching
when I found I could no longer stand

their screeching. Since he arrived, my hearing is not what
it used to be. I find the senseless cries of those
uncivilized birds unbearable – as they find

talkative me. Once he goes, I'll have to find my place again
among my own, go back to playing dumb. Knowing
I cannot stave off the yearning

that will master me for words addictive as grain cracked open
on the tongue. Ashamed, alone again,
I'll start to haunt the beach, waiting for

another to come along, to gift me speech.

The Ultimate Secret

It wasn't after all Snake's tongue but Parrot in disguise.
The hint contained in its whispered cries: *Eve: Eva: Ave.*

Yard Fowl

Rooster

As long as a Rooster somewhere
is angry enough to claw at
the sun blood red rising and
pull it through, day will come:
the world will go on.

Hen

Woman luck lie a dungle heap,
fowl come scratch it up
                    - Jamaican saying

Some find you loud mouth and simple,
for every egg laid a big announcement
            a cackle, some find you
the broody hen, not knowing all
is meant to throw spies off the scent
of your blood's secret: you know
the sky isn't falling, geese don't lay
golden eggs, superior knowledge
resides in the feet.

You are mistress of maps to the under
layer, to buried treasure. Why else
do you nod your head and give thanks
as you sup? With every scratch,
woman's luck you turn up.

Senseh

O for a peel-neck hen, one with
        ruffled feathers, magic in its feet
                to scratch up conjuration.
Defeat
      the enemy.
             One to signal where

the danger lies, so we can root it out
        make fresh breeze blow, allow
              the children to grow.

Ol'people say, every yard must have
a senseh fowl to brings things
into the open, make the wicked pay,
give the people the courage
to try out each new day.

Guinea Hen

In Granny's eyes, our foremost barnyard warrior is not
    after all our fierce Rooster or surly Turkey Gobbler
but mild Guinea Hen, her badge of office her spotted
    feathers. She stands on guard at that barrier they call
Reputation. For Granny explicating the difference
    between Good Girls and Bad always ends her homily
with warning as fact: *Seven year not enough*
    to wash speckle off Guinea Hen back.

When Granny holds up Guinea Hen as the symbol
of spoilt reputation, we study her pattern and interpret
Granny's warning to mean: *Not that you can't do so.*
    Just don't let the world know.
    Never let the spots show.

Owl

"...the Owl was a baker's daughter"
- *Hamlet* IV: 5

Owl isn't a yard dweller though it lives in close proximity,
overlooking house and land from its niche
in the breadfruit tree.

I hardly ever see it. Its presence I sense when the air
seems churned into motion at dusk; a pricking
of the skin signalling

the ghostly hunter on the wing. The world seems shaken
to feel Owl measure out the air into quadrants
for better stalking; sift the night for prey.

To the old people Owl is ill-favoured, rider of nightmares
like half-baked dreams sprinkled
with grave dust.

So why do I on some days awaken to a ghostly presence
which does not leave me with dread
but a half-life

of something soothing and warm-scented, a present of
morning's rising crust:
the fecundity of bread.

HUMMINGBIRD

Your daily stance your warrior pose
against the Sun to vanquish foes.
Your virility glows. For your capoeira
dance, the drum rolls beaten by your heart.

When Sun retires, you too withdraw.

Your heart surprised at sudden rest
can leave you life-less.

Should this be death, you know
you'll rise again on beat of wings
reborn as bird, iridescent dazzler.
But still the warrior that never rests

till day is done, for Sun's the same

and will require your glowing ardour
to light his flame.

Forever combat-ready, dancing now
before the flowers of fire, lancing
the hearts you claim as your
domain: their hidden cache

the elixir of immortality, the honey

reserved for warriors of
Blue-Hummingbird-of-the-Left:
Huitzilopochtli.

WOODPECKER

Women were created from yellow-skin plum trees
transformed by the action of the woodpecker
                    - Amerindian myth

O Miss Yellow-skin Plum, Miss Prune-face,
Miss Disdainful One. Rejecting all suitors.
Still waiting for that magnificent descent
of Woodpeckers!

But times have changed, nuh? So wait on
for the eternally absent, the incomparably
selfish one. Or heed Woodpecker's song,
that barb-tipped tongue:

Plum-tree woman, O my dumb one,
Your secret still sweet as when locked up tight.
My pecker's eternal drumming I cannot disguise,
My need so intense, my greed so unsatisfied,
Perversity my preference now: dead-wood
To wooden bride.

No virgins anymore anywhere.
Woodpecker doesn't care.
He's got what he wanted:
His bright red hair.

O Miss Yellow-skin Plum, Miss Prune-face,
Miss Disdainful One, Miss Wait-a-Bit,
You hear that? You'd better start
transforming yourself.

PARAKEET

I heard a parakeet in the garden
he was talking to Jesus alone
It was Judas betraying the master . . .
          - Jamaican Revival hymn

No longer do we find amusing your surface disguise
as fig- or bulletwood-leaf, as red-peas pod, as unripe mango,
as milk-corn cob. We have learnt how childish chatter can
obscure sinister intention, gregariousness mask selfishness,
mischievousness disguise cunning.

Rejecting flesh, you savage pimento to devour the seeds;
slice into orange for its pips, tear cashew to bits for its kernel.
Nothing is sacred. Yet we have learnt parrot-fashion from
you, a thing or two: how to attack the surface over and over
till we rip it apart, enabling us to reach the entrails, expose
the tatters of this masquerade, this pitchy-patchy Perroquet.
Perroque. Pierrot. Pierre.

Revealing, not Peter, but a Judas here.

MAGPIE

Couldn't you even try to be as easy as neat
as buttoned up as pie with its secrets under cover

no revealing what's concealed till invited? No
spilling out and blabbing to the world (not even

a whisper of four-and-twenty blackbirds baked in –
not before they're summoned to sing). O Magpie,

can't you learn from the very concoction
you've given name to, its lush inside as mixed-up,

as pied as you are, but such tight control, such
a buttoned-down and crusty exterior!

Can't you see how like type out of wack, all pied up,
you gabble words that are senseless? If only

you'd stop and swallow a few before speaking. But no!
Take that back, we shouldn't mention 'swallow'

in your hearing, since your name – 'pica' – has been given
by the medical profession to that obsession with eating

unsuitable objects, such as chalk, clay, or – by those
in that so-called 'delicate way' – pied choices like

green eggs and ham, or chocolate and jelly with lamb
(or anything else that will rhyme in the belly).

You've been accused of 'conspicuous arrogance', greed,
gossip, dissipation, vanity – Bacchus your lord, symbol

of drunkenness and garrulity; of engaging in
'indiscriminate collection' – known as thievery. Even

your name you have plucked from the tongues of
chattering women (also 'pied'); O the poor little

Margaret now forced to be Mag (and fit to be tied!).
You've also been identified with poets though

I myself the connection cannot divine except
perhaps through Bacchus – and a few drops of wine?

Though you might also have been that folk poet
back then, the Pied Piper, that made off

with the children when – imagine the irony –
you're the one who could say on this solitary

occasion: "I wuz robbed." Your reputation needs
rescuing but you make it so hard as I find you

parading in yard after yard in our neighbourhood,
sitting on fences, teasing the dogs, engaging in

seemingly senseless chatter – to divert from
what you plan to nick.

Plus, I do hate talebearers and I've just heard
this trick: that once upon a time when

a couple had to be parted for a while, each
gave the other a mirror. Should one be unfaithful,

that mirror would change instantly into you, Magpie,
and you'd fly straight back to the other – with the news.

O why did I choose to defend such a blabbermouth?
But you simply refuse to be overlooked, you

celebrant of the variegated, the parti-coloured,
mixture of paint, pigment, picture of pied beauty.

For I too am pied. And no one has ever said you've lied.
No hypocrite you, I can relate to that.

No struggle to figure you out. It's obvious as black
and white. Plain as night and day. Easy as pie.

Once upon a time, Peacocks were eaten
      but only by Royalty and therein
            hangs a tale.
King George the Third in a moment of
      lucidity, was set to practicing
            his Speech from the Throne.
All went well, except that at the end of
      every sentence he intoned
            the word: 'Peacock'.
The Minister sent to drill him scratched
      his head and finally said:
            "Majesty, 'peacock'
is a very find word. So fine indeed it
      needs be reserved exclusively
            for Royalty. If you pardon me
- Majesty - such a word should never
      be breathed aloud to excite
            the common herd."
This pleased the king excessively.
      Thereafter his speech he said
            punctuated by the word
'peacock' but silently at the end
      of every sentence. Interpreted
            as a strategic pause
which many said made for an excellent
      delivery. Still, some kept muttering
            'insane'. Not knowing
that in eating peacock, the King
      had swallowed not just bird
            but word.

Which is to say, with the goose: sauce.
With the peacock: sorcery.

The navy from Tarshish arrives with gold and silver,
ivory, apes, and Peacock, with his hundred eyes.

King Solomon brings his children and his hundred wives.
Stretching a mile or so long, they line up on the wharf

to view the strange barbaric throng. Peacock assumes
the reception is for him and almost manages a song.

Peahen, ignored by everyone, dutifully following in his
rhythm, carries the suitcases and a flagon of

smelling salts. Peacock marches up and down and struts
his stuff and preens. Until he fluffs his tail and careens

to the limit of his pride. It is then that Peahen rushes
to his side and hisses in her quiet voice: "Feet! Feet!"

Peacock, as if stung, whimpers and in retreat lowers
his head in shame. Pride falls like his eyes to the ground

and his ugly black feet. Peahen unstoppers the smelling
salts and delivers it neat. Peahen does not consider

herself cruel, or, as some would have it, consumed by
jealousy. Oh no, she says, it's just that a woman's got to

protect the one who puts bread on the table, even from
himself. Nobody looking at him (she says) would suppose

his brain to be the size of a pea, his head so light, all that
arrests his fancy, or even more permanent flight is his

wife – me – having to remind him every time, of those ugly
black feet. The only thing that keeps him grounded – and in line.

ALBATROSS

Long before Copernicus or Galileo
the Albatross had taken the Earth's measure,
surveyed its daily round. It chose the life of
the outsider, putting its trust in the ribbon of winds
girdling the world. Once airborne, the Albatross
turns stateless ocean rover, its impetus born
of knowing that in going forward it will always
be homing back.

EMPEROR PENGUIN

The Emperor Penguin stands sentinel to progeny in the dark
Antarctic winter. Two months solitary on the Great Ice Barrier
incubating a single egg in the fold of the skin between his legs.
By the time his mate returns from her long eating spell
to relieve him, he's but a shadow of his former self.
Such parental cooperation! Sounds to me like a marriage made
in Hell. Penguins perhaps are too well matched. By the time
mating season draws near, the male has forgotten all he's
learnt the previous year. With everyone dressing unisex, he
sometimes presses the wrong suit. The consequences could
be appalling. What does an Emperor Penguin do with no egg
to hatch on the Great Ice Barrier during the dark Antarctic
winter? It seems as if in exchanging wings for flippers, flight
for fortitude, the courageous Emperor Penguin
made a mess of dress.

OSTRICH

Ostrich in forsaking flight for speed, gave up
the empowerment of challenging gravity.
Slick and swift as a steed, its feet are also
weapons: Ostrich can turn vicious.

In choosing Earth, did Ostrich abandon
that loop connecting worlds to indulge
its own base instinct? Or is fight to Earth
the natural pair, as flight to Air?

THE DANCE OF CRANES

Ancient priestesses schooled
        in dance notation
                copied down the mating
dance of cranes to use as blueprints
        for constructing
                labyrinths
so initiates might wind their way to ecstasy.

Cranes
                whose
                                ful
                                joy
        intricate
                dances

                                sum
                        moned
the   spring

        to distant places
                        cranes
                                whose   flight

confounded

        distances
                        and elemental

                                spaces.

Imagine such distance   wound into
such small compass.   The ecstatic
twists and turns   the joyful   leaps
contorted. The   magic   of   the
flight   of cranes   reduced   to an
earthbound   symbol   of souls
finding themselves lost and wingless

2: ISLANDED

O
yes.   So   true,
Your   Majesty.   Round   as
we know God's world to be, O Queen,
without a doubt, Columbus fumbled. Isabella
gingerly taking in her hand his latest gift, the
· black pimento grain brought from her new-found land
rolled one between thumb and finger, inhaled, then
imperiously crushed it, setting free all the spices
- Cinnamon Nutmeg Clove. It totally bowled
her over. Her Exchequer quickly took control.

Spices   worth   their   weight   in   gold

Worlds   to   be   crushed   for

their   spices   their   gold.
O

DISCOVERY

Always
> like the futile march of crab-armies
> from mangrove fortress to the beach

Always
> like the palm-fringe waiting
> to be breached

Already I know, the moment you land
I become islanded

In the shadows of the rain forest
I wait in submission

Amidst the trembling of the leaves
I practice hesitant discourse

Always
> my impenetrable heart.

THE BIRTH OF ISLANDS

Fire at the core
Necklace of ash, stone, coral.
Islands emerge, submerge or shift
with continental drift. Islands
are not immortal. Without you,
islands could never be. You
are the portal. Islands are born
from your longings.

See how easy:
      The spoon stirs up the void
      Seabird drops its egg
      A sand-grain launches itself

You blow breath on the ocean

Something breaks out on the face of the water

MESSAGE IN A BOTTLE

In its daily scouring of the rim of islands
the ocean prays for the invention of
postcards, telephones, E-mail,
transatlantic cables. Tired
of the tedium of reading
bottle mail and its futile blatherings:

> *Under a hostile sun I lie*
>
> . . .
>
> *From islands I want to be free*
>
> . . .
>
> *From savages, rescue me*
>
> . . .

Most times, the ocean can't be bothered
to deliver. Not even one decent poet
among them. The ocean itself can turn savage.

Thirteen Ways of Looking at Blackbird
(after Wallace Stevens)

I
The ship
      trips
into sight of land. Blackbird
is all eyes. Vows nothing but sunlight
will ever hold him now.

II
Survivor of the crossing, Blackbird
the lucky one in three, moves
his eyes and weary
limbs. Finds his wings clipped.
Palm trees gaze and swoon.

III
Swept like the leaves on autumn wind,
Blackbird is bought and sold and bought
again, whirled into waving fields
of sugar cane.

IV
Blackbird no longer knows
if he is man or woman or bird or simply is.
Or if among the sugar cane he is
sprouting.

V
Blackbird's voice has turned rusty.
The voice of the field mice
is thin and squeaky.
I do not know which to prefer.

VI

Blackbird traces in the shadow not cast
the indecipherable past.

VII

Blackbird finds thrilling
      the drum beats drilling
            the feet of
men of women into
      utterance.

VIII

To Blackbird rhythm
      is inescapable
Fired to heights alchemical
the immortal bird consumed

Charlie Parker

wired.

IX

Blackbird once again
attempts flight. Crashes into
the circle's contracting edge.

X

Even the sight of the whip makes
Blackbird cry out sharply.
No euphony.

XI

Pierced by fear, Massa and all his generation
mistake Blackbird for the long shadow.

XII

Blackbird strips to reduce gravity's pull
readying for flight again. Fate hauls him in
to another impetus.

XIII

In the dark
     out of the sun
Blackbird sits
     among the shavings
from the cedar coffins.

MISREADING WALLACE STEVENS

"The birds are singing in the yellow patios"
- Wallace Stevens, "Like Decorations in a
Nigger Cemetery" (1938)

On a day beloved of travel writers
the yellow of tropical, the pale green
palms upturned

the vivid birds preening
in patios overlooking a blue
denial

the world arranged just so
for the viewers.
Unseen

like decorations
in the cemetery right under
their noses

the graves
outlined in white bleached
coral, the conch shells

splayed like bones. Unseen
the mirror's solicitations
to keep the spirits

spellbound; the flowers faded
and torn, the crockery
decorations

broken and worn
like the folk
buried there.

In a moment of heightened interest
in something totally trivial
the visitors

are caught spellbound
by the sound
of a funeral

procession. A brass band.
And a choir of birds singing
in the yellow patois.

How exotic! the travel writers thrill.
How perfectly chic!
Understanding

not a word, they immediately
arrange for translation and
publication – each one

carrying home
a trophy recording and a wonderful
necklace of birds' feathers.

The funeral procession
passes into
the cemetery out of sight.

Unseen the black souls
now dressed
in white

singing in the yellow patois
accenting
towards light

Rejected Text for a Tourist Brochure

"I saw my land in the morning
and O but she was fair"
- M.G. Smith, "Jamaica" (1938)

I

Come see my land

Come see my land
before the particles of busy fires ascend;
before the rivers descend underground;
before coffee plantations
grind the mountains into dust; before
the coral dies; before the beaches
disappear

Come see my land
Come see my land
And know
That she was fair.

2

Up here, the mountains are still clear.
After three weeks, I heard a solitaire.
Down there, the mountains are clear-cut
marl pits. Truckers steal sand from beaches,
from riverbeds, to build another ganja palace,
another shopping centre, another hotel
(My shares in cement are soaring). The rivers, angry,
are sliding underground, leaving pure rockstone
and hungry belly.

3

No Problem, Mon. Come.
Will be one hell of a beach party.
No rain. No cover. No need to bring
your bathing suit, your umbrella.
Come walk with me in the latest stylee:
rockstone and dry gully. Come for the Final
Closing Down Sale. Take for a song
the Last Black Coral, the Last Green Turtle,
the Last Blue Swallow-tail (preserved behind glass).
Come walk the last mile to see the Last Manatee,
the Last Coney, the Last Alligator, the Last Iguana
Smile.

Oh, them gone already? No Problem, Mon.
Come. Look the film here.
Reggae soundtrack and all. Come see
my land. Come see my land and know, A-oh,
that she was fair.

MISSING

The last time I went home they told me you were missing.
For the first time since I'd known myself, you were not
there.

For one so home-bound, who could have foreseen
such a dramatic ending: Missing Person. Presumed Dead.

Village fiddler, your playing was always out of tune.
Your choice of instrument that creaking violin: What

was it signalling? The ne'er-do-well? The one who failed
to make the grade? The only one who stayed?

Yet, your discordant life played out, I was amazed to find
you hadn't passed through like a false note a broken string.

You remained a vibrating source of conversation
an endless susurration. With the police indifferent,

your poverty-stricken neighbours hired a van
to take them on their own investigation across the river

to the rumoured scene of the crime, for they believed
you had been murdered. Theories were rife:

- *You know how he facety when he tek up his waters.*
- *He did get money so he boasy that day.*

Why had you taken that bus at all?
Where were you headed?

In a life devoid of excursions did you know
you were finally setting out to be tripped up by your fate?

Leaving home like that, you have missed so much:
Mass Dick's funeral, Tennie migrating, Pearlie and baby too,

Miss Carmen's husband dead. So many departed.
The young ones sit and wait. Not in the expectation

of any return. Waiting has become an occupation. A
permanent state. Abandonment the theme of this new life.

One day, I thought I heard you, Jumbieman,
unburied wandering spirit playing an unstrung fiddle

headed our way. Miss D who is the oldest person I know said:
Nah, is you hearing bad. Ol'time sinting done weh

Not even duppy bodder wid we now.
Yes, it's Version Time. Lyrics and licks. A life too raucous

for anyone to hear ghostly fiddlers again. Not you.
Not Tambu. Not Jonkannu. Not silenced Gumbay.

O Tambu you come back
but wha de use?
You come back but
wha de use?

HERE AND THERE

I knew I couldn't get there from here. Here
was the edge from which time slipped, objects

disappeared; the road slid from view,
voices sheared off as the paths veered. Here

was the dark, the damp, the steadfast dew,
the blue shadows following the sun as far as

here. Then stopping off to rest too long while
the lightness left, for there. Where was there, then?

Where the sky billowed. Beyond the curve of day.
So what alchemical light came through to point

the way, what magic words for the getaway?
For one day, I walked through without knowing

I had finally chewed into dust and absorbed
into my being the fibres of what it meant to be.

Here.

BLUE

Never knew that blue was a song to be sung,
no, never knew. Thought blue was something
swallowed: a choke, an anguish, an ache,
a separation from everyone, a curtain, an

emptiness, a disappearance. Thought I was
the only person who knew the meaning of blue.
I was very young then: pale, washed out, yet
already too far out to be extracted from indigo.

Thought blue was a lone sound, just one note
banged out on a piano key, in the tapping of
fingers to grate on the nerves, blue was for me,
solo. A game of solitaire, a disaffection.

Blue was like standing on that isthmus between
oceans, finding washed up on the beach
a lone shoe. Blue was not me and you, but me
or you. Avoidance the meaning of 'true blue'.

Blue was that in-betweenness, that moment
of change, of solstice, where you feared to fall
between worlds, into that blue crevice, become lost
in canyons and gullies, snow drift, millennium shift.

Blue was not that everyday gear that you wear:
blue jeans. No, blue was that covering for the
young dead, for the modest: the nuns, the
Virgin Mary, the untouched, the untouchable

life, the one you wanted to escape from, but
how could you? With the blue sky so unreachable,
the blue sea so unreadable, spattered only by flecks
of cloud, of foam like broken promises.

See now the blue smoke rising from morning fires
in the mountain cockpits, ephemeral sign
of the brother you'll set out to meet, to be greeted
instead by the smoke ring of the other: "Me no sen,

yu no come." You'll return to the blue-hollowed hills,
the shadowed evening, the slowing down of pulse
and heartbeat, to await the calling out by passers-by
of the saddest, the bluest, the most contradictory

words in the world: Good Night.

one day, strength (from
where, you don't know) to aim
for the opening, to say: I am leaving.
To walk to the edge of your feeling.
To load up with guilt (not a word
from the ones at the threshold). Not
a word! You keep walking. Down
the dirt track, to the lane, to
the street, to the highways of
the world. You alone. Not yet stunned
by the brightness. Not by hardness
of stone, of the pavement. No.
You say: I could get used
to the lightness.
                    Till the day
you're snared by another sensation:
on a hilltop, at that, you find yourself
drowning, a movement of ebbing
and flowing. You recognize early
(or too late) that you failed to detach
from that mooring.

Always, cruelty of choice.

Here's the knife.

Yourself:
          Executioner
Midwife

Lost Tropic

Friend, I'm in a bad way, my skin
leaches out more tropic every day
like flood-prone mountain soil.

Left behind: uncompromised bones
like volcanic stones on hillsides.
Waiting. For Thunder.

Today, though, no rain. The Sky Shepherds
have corralled their flocks.

BLUE MAGIC CARPET

Driving up
>>> mountain trails
>>>>>> to Cinchona

I'm not feeling
>>> the punishment
>>>>>> of that dirt track

I'm not watching
>>> the curves
>>>>>> nothing scares me

nothing
>>> not the precipice
>>>>>> falling away

look way down
>>> not altitude
>>>>>> look up there

nothing scares me in these mountains
>>> not even
>>>>>> you leaving

to rock bottom I've fallen already
>>> see down there
>>>>>> through undergrowth

dark as umbra
>>> look down

Then at the last bend
        as we enter the garden slowing down
            by the sinister Blue Gum

Look Up!
        The tone of your voice makes me look
              Can't stop

going Oh!
        I'd forgotten Agapanthus
            Hydrangea

famed blue hillside at Cinchona in May every year
        Now I'm touched
            Is that why you brought me

5000 feet plus
        up here?

Can't stop leaping out to fall on this carpet:
Agapanthus   Hydrangea. It's the acid that
does it turns it blue they all say. Can't stop
my own acid leaching away. To blue up
this carpet some more

Thinking   (for the first time in my life)
Thinking   I'm going to be alright
Thinking   The higher I climb the sweeter the air
Thinking the blues are getting lighter year by year.

MOON

I'm walking on this dark path overhung with hibicus,
bougainvillea, when suddenly, an opening to the sky,
and in my face, this great, big, overpowering moon, in
silver. Thank you, Moon, for showing your most dazzling
self tonight, dimming the stars, seducing me from gloomy
thoughts, from citylight. I know it's your best face because
each month I watch you grow fat, then waste away on
some celestial diet before you disappear. No mystery
there. I know your ways. Soon a new you so svelte and
trim will start coming round again – until you lose control
and gorge to almost bursting. I can tell by your patina
on what you are feasting. This month it's the metallic you,
with hint of quicksilver, pewter, antimony. At other times,
there's the warmth of liquid amber, of honey. Though you
have never failed us yet, you tantalize with the uncertainty
of never knowing how big you'll get. That makes you
almost human. Not like that Sun who acts as if he's so
divine. I know comparisons are odious, dear Moon,
but such self-discipline is hard to stomach. He comes
showing the same predictable face day after day: no fat,
no shrinkage, no blemish. He does get a bit red and
wobbly some afternoons (bad-minded people say, from
drink!). I'd like to think it's just that sometimes the old
fuddy-duddy can't wait till he's out of sight to change into
his old red flannel shirt and relax. By doing a two-step.

WILD NESTER

Wild nester, wild nester so far from home
Wish I had the wings of a dove
                            - Traditional song

I   Wild Nester

By ones, by twos, the travellers return from winter faring,
their dress so elegant, their bearing like doctors
on their rounds checking me out to see
that all is not just well but as they left it. I feel them
soundlessly berate me with a look, criticize with a nod
between them: Why did she limb that tree? How goes
the Venerable Oak? How dare she suppress
Virginia Creeper's growth?

These birds I do not know as they do not know me; my
city backyard too confined for ceremonial introductions.
How I miss that vireo who shamelessly on arrival in the south
each June leaves everywhere amongst the leaves, its vulgar
and highly embellished calling card:

John Chew- it
John Chew- it
Sweet John Chew- it
Swe-et John   Swe-et John   Swe-et John

Faced with these northern scrutineers I ask myself: What
is the secret of making them yield their names, here in a foreign
land with no one over backyard fences to ask anything.
No Unka to whistle bird-calls. No Syl to tease.
No Jerry in the schoolyard to imitate the shy Mourning Dove.
No Bobby with his springe to capture Bald Pate.
No parrot in a cage to say even "Pretty Please."

No familiar Island Mockingbird to interweave with its soaring imitative songs just a hint of its own troubles:

See me leg See me leg
Pain Pain Pain Pain Pain

None to give out a name.

II   *Ping*

                    Ya!

No Chicken Hawk to bait me while
next door my playmates sing

Bluebird Bluebird in and out the window
To see a rose again

Teasingly calling over the fence:

Buddy, Buddy come play with me
Put down your books and play with me

"No, I can't play I have to stay a yard
to keep Hawk from Auntie's Chickens."

Ping!

Primly. And pleased as puss that I'm
so important. They laugh. 'Chicken Merry
Hawk Deh Near' – like Auntie – I warn them

'Go weh' they cry and go back
to their playing. Soon my yard
feels too quiet

Ya!

Suddenly in the sunhot I shiver.
Auntie would say: Somebody's walking
on your grave, girl. Auntie knows
everything. But Auntie's not here.

Ping Ya!

Auntie's far away. Shh! Mother Hen's
shushing her chickens. Shh!
The beat of wings?

      Ping Ya!

A shadow growing

      Ping Ya!
Chicks freezing
   playmates' voices
      across the fence

Put down your books and play with me

I try to answer

                Ping Ya!

But it's seizing

  my voice

    my heart is

      its wings are

O Chicken Hawk
what will Auntie say? (I only
have time to think)

before

                              Ping!

            Ya!
Ping

III   Blue Quit

In Sweetwater Woods now
the Pea-doves are nesting

Across the blue water
my life is on hold

So what would I trade
to return to that place
to the blue hills, the hollows,
and bold Mistress Blue Quit
gossiping in the glade:

- *Sairey coat blue*
- *A true?*
- *True Blue!*

Hear her husband nuh, good for
nothing but nodding in the shade:

For true. For true. For true.

IV   *White Belly*

      and sometimes I'm that querulous
complaining White Belly Dove
and you its eternal interrogator:

- *Rain come wet me Sun come bun me O!*

  Why don't you build a house?

- *What's it to you?*

Yes,
What's it to you?

Sometimes I press my hands on the
top of my head to hold the lid on.
Tight. To keep the stories from spilling,
words from leaping into the glare of an
indifferent light. In Cockpit Country
deep caverns, dark secrets, blue endings
even now: *What Woodpecker say in him belly
hard fe ansa.*

For true. For true. For true.

V   *Blue Foot Traveller*

That world no longer exists.
Yet from the architecture of longing
you continue to construct a bountiful edifice.

This is not exile.
You can return any day to the place that you came
from
though the place you left has shifted a heartbeat.

Like that artful dove Hopping Dick
you hopscotch.

3: PENNY REEL

WITH MY LITTLE EYE . . .

I spy

a ribbon like a rainbow that loops out
and in like the dance round the Maypole
in the schoolyard. Girls to the left boys
to the right as weaving in and out we
make a basket. Skirts flashing, hair flying
for we've left it undone, turned it loose
– like the witches – to snare someone.

> Not knowing then, in the schoolyard by the sea
> that Death was that kindly old man
> who sat by the shore splitting reeds to weave
> his basket to capture fish
>
> that give the wrong answer

Little fishes in the schoolyard
skipping rope, looping rhymes:
              Little Sally Water
Hide and Seek
London Bridge is Falling Down
O the See-Saw
the Merry-Go-Round
swinging in the air, knowing
        the pendulum that swings always
                                    stops.

> Then scurries back here.

With my little eye, what did I spy?

All passed through my mind then
like thread through the needle's eye
for nothing was I ready to see.

RIDDLE

Together, babe, we could have had the world sewn up.
You filled my eye, I kept you in stitches. When we
moved together we glided – no hitches. Yes, sometimes
I needled you. Too pushy, you claimed. But you – so
spineless, so easy, you always needed me to drag you
through. Yet, life's so unfair. For I'm the one left empty,
threadbare. While you, Mr. Sleazy, without me to keep you
on the straight and narrow, you still manage to thread your
way, tying everything – as you did me – up in knots.

EMBROIDERY

The women of the family took tea all together except for
Aunt Millie, Uncle Vincent's wife. She read books, she

wore makeup and jewellery even on weekdays. On Sunday
afternoons behind locked door, she had me put colouring

(Madame Walker's, IMPORTED FROM AMERICA) in her
hair. She was a blue foot, a stranger, not a born-ya. She

had crossed water. They did not know precisely where
Uncle V had found her. He was the eldest, family head.

A sly dog and purse-string controller, so no one said
anything. Aunt Millie smiled often but her mouth was

sewn up. Her reticence offering them few strands,
the women of the family enhanced them with embroidery

(washing lightly in vinegar to keep the colours fast). From
her straight nose and swarthy skin they plucked skeins

to compose the features of a Jewess, or herring-bone in
the outside daughter of a rich merchant or plantation owner.

Her mother was someone mysterious, whipped onto the
scene with a slanting backstitch. She once sang opera?

She was said to be of Panamanian or Colombian origin.
Something exotic enough – like a french knot – to mistrust

but work in. They reviled Aunt Millie's use of scent. From
the few words they extracted they thought they detected

a foreign accent. Sometimes they feathered in 'Haitian',
infilled with dark threads to signify the occult powers

of that nation – how else could she have snared such as
Uncle V? They thought she kept her distance because

she was all of the above and snobbish. *My dears, such airs!*
She and I were *What a pair!* Myself, orphaned with frayed

edges unravelling into their care. Everyone knowing my
pathetic history, I could wind myself up in Aunt Millie's

mysterious air, undulate in the sweet waves (artificially
induced) of her hair. She nurtured me on books and

reticence. The women of the family fed me cold banana
porridge (or so everything then seemed) told me tales

of girls who did and men who didn't marry them. Tried to
enmesh me in their schemes to undo Aunt Millie's disguise.

In the end they embroidered her an elaborate cover when
(I could have said) a plain winding sheet would have suited her.

For to me she gave her story, unadorned. The women of
the family willed me their uniform tension. Aunt Millie left

me her pearls. I sold them, became a blue foot traveller.
Kept no diary. Sewed up my mouth. Shunned embroidery.

PENNY REEL

It is Saturday, the night of penny reel dances, girls in
pressed hair, white muslin and sashes, turn to
high-stepping gentlemen as they weave out and in
eye passing each other on the go-round.

The little dressmaker in the circle of light spilled from
Home Sweet Home lamp shade, sits sewing
at her straight-stitch treadle-foot machine, unwound
by the laughter, the fiddle and fife of penny reel.

Near the very same spot on the edge of the park where
the stark shanty-town edges in, there's
a Merry-go-Round. Her children she locks up inside
and away from temptation till she earns

enough pennies for their ride. She's not locked in.
It's life she's locked into. Can't remember
how she entered that ring. Can't see the revellers.
In a tenement room, there're no windows to outside:

every door in a row facing in. No wheel and spin.
The treadle-foot machine the go-round she rides.
But sometimes (she's noticed of late)
there's slippage, as with silk from her customers,

easy slide of her body to a pull from the outside.
Alone save the children, how unattached she feels.
Out there, her Saturday night sisters weave
something from life. Each reel a new set so the dance

might continue. Who decides on our measure?
She addresses this to no one in particular.
Her man could be anywhere: penny-reeling,
at his gambling, the rum-bar. Perhaps (she is hopeful)

tonight he won't come. Forever. No more scars
on her body criss-crossing like ribbons. No more
riding her. No more grinding her down. No more
turning her into Ol'Higue. If she knew how to stop

> having children she'd do it. But there's no one to ask.
> Her sisters are all at the dance. Penny reel.
> Thread reels her in. Three a.m. and she's
> sewing for a Sunday delivery. Though the fabrics

are dancing, kaleidoscoping her eyes, her feet keep on moving
the treadle. Up and down. O Saturday night sisters moving out
and in to that rhythm of life.
But like her customers,

> they too dissolve in her mind into parts custom fitted,
> tape ribbon the only measure she knows.
> And she? Do they see her as more
> than a figure kneeling down to adjust the hems

of their garments, straight pins in her mouth. Do they know
she is coming unstitched? Sometimes
they don't pay her on time. Sometimes never.
And there's that Merry-go-Round. If she knew

> how to rain curses down she would do it. But there's
> no one to ask how to creep into houses, rip
> their clothing to strips, tie as ribbons to the maypole,
> and swing. If only she knew how to stop herself

wanting to fly through the walls as her feet work
the treadle. If only she could stay plaited up
like the ribbons round the pole. Stop reeling off
into this other. Not the straight-stitcher looking after

the children but the one overlooking. The one
who rips her skin, strips and discards it, so that
bat-like, taking wing, she flies through the air,
homing only to sound, to movement, the scent

of the dancers O my sisters who are reeling. She dives
for their blood. To suck up their being.
But the ribbons criss-crossed at the pole
are unyielding to witches or to humans

who ribbon their skin. And because it is Saturday evening
the one time in the week these lassies and lads
are not grieving for homes left behind. Freed
from labour, from tenement rooms, they abandon

themselves to each other. Keep dancing
till the dawn when witches must return to their skin.
Or be undone. Like the man coming in to curse her
– 'Ol'Higue' – when she asks where he's been.

For its dawn. She needles him with her eyes.
If she knew how to kill she'd do it but there's
no one to ask. Her sisters still dancing. She finds herself
knotting a thread round his neck. She jerks it. Bites.

There, it's done. But it's only one garment. Many more
till delivery. Sunday morning soon come.
Thank God for the dawning and the whisper
in the streets of the revellers passing, the girls

in crushed muslin, their hair now unpressed, the boys
still high-stepping. Easy passage tonight.
They have paid for the ride.
O penny reel dancers unreeling.

White

"Take me and make me whiter than snow"
                - Protestant hymn

Nothing comes white here naturally, not unless
you count sea foam or cloud cap-in-hand begging
passage across the blue immensity. No snow-
scapes, sheep don't roam through here. Heaven
is where you have to go to become whiter than
snow. Or so they sing in the chapel. Try telling that

to Miss Dora the laundress who soaks clothes
overnight to let them know who is mistress then
beats them on the big rock and hangs them on
the bush to bleach in the dew. No speck permitted
to pass through her needle-eye scrutiny; the whites
she dips in a rinse of laundry blue to purge them

as sinners do with hyssop. Starch from cassava
grain Miss Dora uses to stiffen the clothes against
the playfulness of breeze that might see them
at their ease on the clothes-line and come tek fass
and undress them. Every weekday, Miss Dora's
laundry stays stiff and upstanding on the line,

like flags, in glorious array like cherubim and
seraphim, though Miss Dora don't business with that.
If you try to tell her that Heaven is the place to go
to climb the golden stair, turn sheep in the
shepherd's flock, become whiter than snow, she
will bridle and say, so what wrong with my big rock,

since when you dissatisfy with clothes scrub
on this washboard in tin tub, then how come you
never tell me you don't like how I starch, how I iron,
till now you have to go to some far away place
to obtain satisfaction? No, Miss Dora, you explain
(for Sunday being her rest day she has never

darkened church door), is skin we talking about.
If sin wash away in Heaven sinners come whiter
than snow. That's how it go. "Hm. Never seen,"
she will say, "what they call snow or sheep. Some
speak of white foam on the sea but poor me never
been there yet. Plus if I was to leave the clothes

dirty, go walk bout, inspect the whole world, like
them bothersome young girls nowadays, what
those fine folk in the church would have to wear
come Sunday? Who to wash, starch and iron
the frills, who to stiffen the shirt collar, lay
the peplum straight, crease the pleat, who to make

even the worst sinner look neat and tidy as they
approaching what they call mercy seat, as they
walk up to this Heaven, fall in with the flock?
And another thing: Is this black skin I been living in
from I born. From morning, as you know,
the one thing I learn good is laundering. That

mercy seat, that heaven for me is the day I retire
from the work and put up my feet. So tell me
why I would suddenly want to be climbing up
golden stair, join some flock of sheep the first
time I setting eye on them. And when I get there,
why I would suddenly want my skin to turn white

as this shirt I just done wring out, start look like
that sheet on the line? If ever I should arrive at
them high-up place there, as a good washer
woman I couldn't hold mi tongue, I would
duty bound to say, Lord, I glad I reach but I have
to beg you Sar, please go easy with the bleach."

LACEMAKER
Valenciennes, 1794

Attached to my bobbins like the spider
I, with no time on my hands, spin out
a lifeline to hang on. Then I make
the noose: to form the hole I capture air
tangible as breath in this damp cellar. Round it,
I weave the thread in finest silk which will age
(unlike me) to palest cream, ecru, ivory,
age into 'charming old lace'.

I envy the spider her speed. In inches my life
edges by – (Her Ladyship so many yards for her ruff,
My Lord, years of work for each cuff, My Lord Bishop
three-quarters of my life to trim his alb).

Like the spider I grow brittle and dry,
like its web (pale and strong) my lace
(kept moist for good tension) surges on
fine as foam on the ocean which I'll never see.

For my eyesight's opalescent as shell now,
my vision translucent as pearl
yet my skeletons of thread stay delicate as webs
(like the fly, it's the holes I'm mesmerized by).

When I die, I'll go to my grave in coarse linen,
no edging. But my virginal hands will not cease
from signing *punto in aria*: stitches in air.
Never cease from making nooses for My Lord, My Lady.

Meantime, the spider and I wait
for our traps to be sprung

for lace-trimmed heads
to swing in bloodied air

(What a waste
of good lace

What a waste
of my lifetime).

PEARL DIVER
Isla de Margarita, 1628

Full fathom five
– or ten, my father
will dive from an open boat
each day. His body
is greedy for water.
Each night, he's caged
in a pen to keep him
chaste and dry as
the biscuits he's fed on.
No woman to stir him,
no water to wallow in;
were he to swallow a drop
next day he'd float like cork,
not go under. Be off our roster,
says Friar Antonio.
He'd never again
go down to the depths
to bring up Ave Maria
bring up sweet
Pater Noster.

Some days, no matter
how hard he plunges
my father surfaces
empty. Friar Antonio
calls it an insult
to Our Maker, caused
by thoughts of sin
(wet dreaming) and
has him whipped.

My father knows
the luck of the dive.
The only thing certain
is that till he dies, each day
he'll fall overboard
as the dew falls
into the open mouth
of the oyster.

BASKETMAKER

Already bestowed the accolades that mark you expert,
you still make baskets for the ordinary: the satchels,
the boxes, the quivers and fans that people need.
For each one marks a step on the journey to perfection,
the reeds in your hand a weave of your post-mortem fate,
each twist of your wrist a template of your soul's
patterning, your craft that will bear you up to the place
where the past masters dwell with the Divine Bird
of the Dawn.

Your hands cannot rest. After death you are still
compelled to weave as you navigate the final passage
where the dread Frog Mistress of Earth, arbiter of your fate,
scrutinizes every twist and turn. You could work
yourself up into such a state. But your entire life has led
you to this moment and as you weave your way your
course is set. Warp becomes worth. In twill and twist
of reeds you know you must entwine the divine, the
labyrinth unwind.

BIRD-MAN / BIRD-WOMAN

Over time, representations of the bird-shaman in pre-Colombian gold work evolved into heart-shaped icons.
- Gerardo Reichel-Dolmatoff, *Goldwork and Shamanism*

It takes heart to become one, the courage to be, to accept the separation from whatever life you embark from: the you who was never completed, the you who was never really there, the you now ripe for transformation into pure spirit of air. But first, in that extremity of solitude that is itself the first test, there is the you who have been chosen to endure the fortress of cold, the fiery furnace; the you who must fast to near-death; the you who must gorge on sacred tobacco juice day after day till the visions come easy; the you who must accept your terrifying gift of fore-seeing as the price of ecstasy; the you who at great risk must intuit and tame your guardian spirit; forge from bird song and calabash, feathers and spit, the implements of your sacred calling; the you who must practice hiring out your voice in the service of animals who will return it unrecognizably coarse but unsurpassed in its versatility; the you who must hang nine nights from the tree. At the end of all this suffering, you'll find the Spirit Death alone come to bear you away. But trust me. Purified, you will rise again another day as that other being, the one destined to serve, destined to cure, destined to recover lost souls, destined, Poet, to sing. But first, soul traveller, you have one more test to meet. Flight as the only way home. Come. The first lesson: how to fold your wings into a heartbeat.

ODE TO PABLO NERUDA*

I
You did say:
Don't call up my person
  I am absent.

But your signs are still decipherable in the pure stone,
in water, in the palm-prints of the labourer. And by those
who like me seek the pure voice untrammelled, the courage
to speak of things nobler than the self, to write impure poetry
that bears witness to the raw and the natural, to be *the voice*
from the bottom of the well.

I want to pay homage but here in the north,
separated by a continent from Santiago, Isla Negra,
or my own island home, so far from the sea I can't strike
the right chord; the measure that I tread moves no one else.
I find myself drifting and wordless.

So I turn to find again something you said
about grasping poetry like thread?
Here it is:

You must spin it
fly a thread
and climb it . . .

This isn't a matter
for deliberation
it's an order.

* *Neruda's words are in italics*

But away from the elements of which my life has been spun
I can't even remember what the knot stands for
that I'm feeling in the thread that fills my hand now.
The thread tying up the bundle of How-It-Was. The thread
that I cling to though you've said poetry is of the here-and-
now *revived by the light of each new day.*

The here-and-now eludes me and I worry about clinging
too tightly to this thread. For what happens if it becomes
too knotted to decipher, too clotted with blood, with mud
from the traveller, too broken to tie again, too ravelled,
too threadbare?

What if you use it all up – for a clothesline that breaks,
for a leash the dog runs off with? What if there's no thread
left? And no more where it came from? There, I've said it.
What if you confidently go to bed leaving a spindle of new
thoughts to be processed. Next morning you reach for the
thread and it's gone like smoke – it's cobweb you're left with.

So Pablo Neruda, although I absolutely agree with many
things you have said this thing with the thread I find a bit
slippery as if you'd reeled it off without thinking and simply
disappeared leaving in the blue this monstrous kite

and me
the one
holding
the string.

2

This thread of poetry: Where does it come from?
Are you born with it? Is it handed to you like a sweet
or a rattle to a child, who takes it without thinking?
As I took your kite string?

Here's how I see it: This thread is one that crosses your path
like the spider's web. You walk through unaware
The Great Spider still clings to it. So now Spider clings
to you, my friend. This is not an accident. You have been
chosen Spider's apprentice. To master language. As
Trickster, to spin and weave tales. To prophesy and heal.
The go-between serving earth and sky. Sometimes the
messenger left dangling.

After you have taken the thread – the thread you cannot refuse
– you must choose how to handle it. You might cut off bits
to skip rope with or play cat's cradle. That's fine for joy
needs to unwind. But there comes a time when you might be
forced to confess: I don't know what I did with the rest of it.

For one day – it's like that scenario that tantalizes in our
nightmares, only this one is real – one day, you are caught
in a dragnet. After your arrest you are brought to account
before some tribunal that will throw the book at you charging
you with theft.

Of what? You will ask. And Neruda will reply: For not
repaying your debt of poetry to the people who forged you
your good life with their blood and their sweat.
All you had to do was weave the thread
into cloth
for those who have
only rags,
nets

for fishermen . . .
and a flag
for each and every one.

You may plead Not Guilty. But perhaps you have already
been weighed and found wanting:
There are some poets so big
they don't fit in doorways
and some merchants so sharp
they don't remember being poor.

If found unconvincing you'll be disconnected, cast away.
Alone, you're left knotted up and wordless.

3
Here's the real trick (and no one ever tells you this):
The thread of poetry to safely travel, the knot of yourself
you must first unravel.

You have to bathe in your own grave
and from the enclosing earth
take a look upward at your pride...
Then, you learn to measure
You learn to speak, You learn to be.

Stripped
and skeletal
you first
navigate
the crawl-space
that allows you
to enter
the labyrinth

blindly
you must
trace every inch
of the root's meander
the convolutions
of the vine
the veined stem

you must take the measure
of the thread born from root
reed stem or fleshy leaf

the thread purged of sap or resin
retted
scourged and riven
to expose its gut.

Immersed
in water
to cast off
impurities

its fibrous heart
elucidated

its old skin shed

you'll
encounter

the thread

born again

as sinews of rope
its tensile strength
corded

The thread that can now
be woven
into strong linen

Like jute fibre
meshed into string

Or like reeds, criss-crossed
into sound centered
at the cross-roads
where the crack
of the whip now
deflects evil forces
clears a path.

If you find yourself
back here
You have mastered
the first trick.

You
can make your way
through the needle's eye
pulled up
by the thread
of your poem

dragged down
by the weight
of words
waiting
to be strung.

The real apprenticeship
has begun.

4
So this knot that I've been feeling, this pearl of anxiety
I'll make part of this rosary of the Alpha and Omega
which could serve as the necklace for Brahma
for Buddha Muhammed the Virgin Mary for Oya.

But really it need not be more than my simple mnemonic
to remind of that journey I myself took long ago through
the roots through the vines. The songs of the heartwood,
the calligraphy of the veins of the leaves almost lost in my
meanderings.

I needed, Neruda, this kite-string to jerk me back to the
source of creation, to that mantra of obligation

A chain-link of miles strung out across oceans
a creole spider-work of many hands.

The beads telling not decades but centuries.

Like this strand of those ancestors handed a one-way
passage to the clearing-house for the convict, the criminal
and cut-throat, the patriot and the rebel,
the pious pilgrim, the debtor, the poor, the downtrodden,
the foolish, the brave heart, the no-hope younger son.
A lifeline to the plantations – the only one other than

swinging as seaman, as buccaneer, as pirate from the rigging, the
yard-arm, the gallows.

Here's a bead
for the spirit necklace
of that other lineage.
The ones bound in chains
dragged across the Atlantic
in vessels, full-rigged.
Their vocal chords ripped
with their names
on the tips of their tongues.
Washed away in salt water
the cartography of home.

Survivors of these crossings transplanted shoots, planted
their children's navel cords to become
the roots and the vines for my string.

And a special bead
for a few I never knew:
the ones who flew
the ones who didn't touch salt
so stayed fluid as air
light as the web of the spider.
Flew back on the wings
that they wove from obligation
pulled by the strings
of ancestral desire.

But the ones that will never die out are too gelatinous
to be strung, being seaweed themselves like floating
sargassos on the currents of life. Spirit pirates with no roots
of their own. The same ones who forged the chains of
indenture, brokered sugar cane sweetened with slave blood.

Their tentacles still as far-reaching and fatal as the
entanglements of the constrictor of vegetal growth: the
Strangler Fig.

So much more unstated as my legacy. Not found in my
blood but possessing me. The fibres of belonging to this world.

5
I've had to weave a cloth to wrap it all up in, a bundle for
carrying for I'm travelling too. But not flying – too much salt
in my veins.

I've been seeking a thread to tie up the bundle which has been
growing unwieldy with the cries and the whispers of the ones
I can't name: The lost ones, the limboed, the un-cared for,
the un-loved. The mortified, the discarded, the 'disappeared'.
All resting uneasy on my conscience. Along with the poems
I failed to deliver or neglected to write and not
saying: "I love you" enough.

Yes, we each have our measure, and our burden to carry
but sometimes the cries are so piercing, we are silenced.

And
there
are
times
like this
when
having
crossed
the abyss
I want
to feel
free

to fly
kites
if I wish
or just
dangle
from
a thread
like
the
spider.

So I'm seeking that old woman, the wizard of the cords
who used to tie up the wind with three knots in a bundle
and sell it to sailors: "Mark well, my good man. Loosen
this knot for light breezes, this one to send you clipping along
and this – woe betide – for a battering."

Yes, I let loose the hurricane. And I'm sorry about the
damage but I forgot which knot was which – that's the
problem with raw thread it – all looks the same. But my
hurricane heart feels better for its roaring, for scouring
the world. For it's the strong wind that cleanses, that
unburdens and purifies. It uplifted the fallen. And broke
the thread. But I'll mend it and restring with fresh beads.

6
I wanted more than woman's knotted portion so I refused
to learn the way of thread: sewing, embroidery, darning,
weaving, tapestry, knitting or crochet do not appear on my CV.

But look at this:

In the sky

a kite
still aloft
and the one
holding
the thread
is me.

Maybe I'll accept after all my commission as apprentice Spider
who spins from her gut the threads for flying,
for tying up words that spilled, hanging out tales long
unspoken, reeling in songs, casting off dances.
And perhaps for binding up wounds?

With strips and remnants left over (and with bits and pieces
of this kite I'm reeling in) I can make a costume for the
dancing fools the masqueraders who dress in rags and tatters

Egungun
Jonkonnu
Pitchy-Patchy
Pierrot and Gombay

the ones who dance the ancestors.

Perhaps when they dance they'll let the wind spin their strips
and their tatters into thread flying ready to be climbed.

Or feather them into birds on the ascendant, their wings
lightly stirring up the ocean below the Middle Passage.

Perhaps they'll spin off into rainbow-hued streamers
plummeting the spaces of Earth into which all those
millions 'disappeared'

Awaking and setting free the dreamers.

For sometimes

It's hard to tell
if we close our eyes or if night
opens in us other starred eyes,
if it burrows into the wall of our dream
till some door opens.

7
And so, my trickster powers evolving, I'm learning like you,
Pablo Neruda veteran tightrope walker, to swing more easily
between joy and obligation.

Here it is: this poem I've made for you like a quilt from thread
and strips as a way of thanking you – not for all your other gifts
(for that would require a book) – but simply
in exchange for your kite which – as you have seen – I've
turned to good use.

And for allowing me to explore boundlessness.

For witnessing how the thread of poetry can serve for
binding up and for un-binding. And for the bounty of these
lines which have unwound themselves.

8
"God is dead," wrote Nietzsche.
"Heaven is empty,"
wrote Kandinsky.
"God is dead."

You, Pablo Neruda,
saw instead

The heavens
unfastened
and open.

NOTES

"Wild Nester" (p. 65)
The words in Italics are songs and sayings from the oral culture of Jamaica and the popular interpretations of bird calls.

Wild Nester - White Belly (p. 71)
The Cockpit Country (also referred to as 'the cockpits' - in 'Blue' p. 61) refers to a geographical region in Jamaica of eerie and unusual landscape developed in limestone (called karst by geologists).

"Penny Reel" (p. 80)
Penny reel = dancing round the Maypole, popular in bygone days in the colonies, derived from the European May Day phallic ribbon dance round a pole. In Jamaica, in working class districts where it became a popular social pastime, dancers paid for each 'reel' or turn at plaiting and unplaiting the ribbons round the pole, hence 'penny reel'. "Penny Reel O" is also the title of a once-popular sexually suggestive folk song.

Ol'Higue = a witch who sheds her skin at night and flies in the shape of a bat to feast on blood. She must assume her skin (and human shape) before daybreak. The term 'Ol'Higue' is also applied to someone perceived as a nag.

"Basketmaker" (p. 90)
In Warao culture (tropical South America), expert basket makers are believed to have a specially reserved place in the after-life, once they have passed a final post-mortem test of their skills.

Ode to Pablo Neruda

Sources of Neruda quotes (in order of appearance in text in Italics):

p. 92 "Don't call . . . absent." (no llames a mi pecho, estoy ausente.) From Luis Poirot, *Pablo Neruda: Absence and Presence,* trans. Alastair Reid (New York: W.W. Norton, 1990), 14.

p. 92 "the voice...well" (La tiranía corta la cabeza que canta, pero la voz en el fondo del pozo vuelve a los manantiales secretos de la tierra y desde la oscuridad sube por la boca del pueblo.) From Luis Poirot, *Pablo Neruda: Absence and Presence*, trans. Alastair Reid (New York: W.W. Norton, 1990), 68.

p. 92 "You must spin it . . . climb it" (tienes que hilarla, levanta un hilo, súbelo) From *Selected Odes of Pablo Neruda*, "Ode to Thread," trans. Margaret Sayers Peden (Berkeley: University of California Press, 1990), 61.

"This isn't . . . order" (No se trata de consideraciones: son órdenes) From *Selected Odes of Pablo Neruda*, "Ode to Thread," trans. Margaret Sayers Peden (Berkeley: University of California Press, 1990), 65.

p. 95 "revived . . . each new day", (lo revive la luz de cada día). From *Selected Odes of Pablo Neruda*, "Ode to Thread," trans. Margaret Sayers Peden (Berkeley: University of California Press, 1990), 67.

p. 94-5 "into cloth . . . every one." (ropa para los que no tienen sino harapos, redes para los pescadores . . . y una bandera para todos.) From *Selected Odes of Pablo Neruda*, "Ode to Thread," trans. Margaret

Sayers Peden (Berkeley: University of California Press, 1990), 63.

p. 95 "There are some . . . poor." (Hay unos poetas tan grandes que no caben en una puerta y unos negociantes veloces que no recuerdan la pobreza.) From *Extravagaria*, "Not quite so tall," trans. Alastair Reid (Austin: University of Texas Press, 1993), 53.

p. 95 "You have to bathe .. . . to be." (Hay que darse un baño de tumba y desde la tierra cerrada mirar hacia arriba el orgullo. Entonces se aprende a medir. Se aprende a hablar, se aprende a ser.) From *Extravagaria*, "Not quite so tall," trans. Alastair Reid (Austin: University of Texas Press, 1993), 53.

p. 103 "It's hard to tell . . . door opens." (No se sabe si cerramos los ojos o la noche abre en nosotros ojos estrellados, si cava en la pared de nuestro sueño hasta que abre una puerta.) From *Fully Empowered*, "In the Tower," trans. Alastair Reid (New York: New Directions, 1995), 25.

p. 103 "between joy and obligation." (entre la dicha y la dureza.) From *Fully Empowered*, "Summary," trans. Alastair Reid (New York: New Directions, 1995), 121.

p. 104 "The heavens . . . open" (el cielo desgranado y abierto) From *Selected Poems*, "Poetry," trans. Alastair Reid (London: Penguin, 1975), 217.

Acknowledgements

Earlier versions of poems in *Over the Roofs of the World* appeared in the following publications:

Matrix, Arc (Canada); *The Sunday Observer* (Jamaica), *The Caribbean Writer* (US Virgin Islands), *Calabash, Obsidian III* (USA), *Poetry London Newsletter, Poetry International 1998* (South Bank Centre), *Agenda, Poetry Wales* (UK); *Kunapipi* (Denmark) 30th International Poetry Festival (with Dutch translations), Rotterdam, and the website www.poetryinternational.org. "White," "Rooster," "Hen," "Guinea Hen," and "Leaving Home" were commissioned by the Commonwealth Institute, London, for an Internet Poetry Residency on the Commonplaces web site in 1999 and were posted on the site.

Poems also appeared in *The New Exeter Book of Riddles* edited by Kevin Crossley-Holland and Lawrence Sail (UK: London, Enitharmon) 1999 and *For the Geography of a Soul: Emerging Perspectives on Kamau Brathwaite*, edited by Timothy J. Reiss. Trenton, NJ: Africa World Press, 2001.

"Ode to Pablo Neruda" was commissioned by BBC Radio 3 for the *Poets Fan Mail* series and first broadcast on October 16, 1997. It was revised for the book. Poems have also been broadcast on the CBC (Canada) and Channel 4 (London).

Much of this volume was written while I was Writer in Residence at the University of Alberta, Canada. I would like to thank the University and the Department of English, especially Steve Slemon, JoAnne Wallace and Kristjana Gunnars. Special thanks to Andrew and Sheila Masson, Janice

Williamson and Lyndal Osborne for Edmonton hospitality. Acknowledgements too for the assistance of Stewart Brown, Victor Chang, Kwame Dawes, Mark McWatt and Denise DeCaires Narain Gurnah. And a special thank you to my editor, Paul Vermeersch.